DIRTY FEMINISM

BY LASHUNTRICE

For that special guy…you've been blessed
For the women that understand
For myself… as a reminder of who I am

Poems

Part One

Part 2

Crooked Crown

You gotta watch where you walking

Shit be real

This is my sidewalk

My walkway

My road to success

I'll push you out the way

So don't get in the way

You gotta watch where you sit

This is my table

My chairs

Decorations laid out for me

My name at the centerpiece

Only my friends joining me

Don't play with me

I'll call security

You gotta watch who you try to control

Not all of us will fold

This is my life

I live how I want to live

My bills

I handle my responsibilities

You can't push me around

You can trash my name in the streets

Try to get others to hate me

But we all see through your insecurities

You gotta watch whose crown you think needs
fixing

And fix your own first

Her
Cheating Man
My
One Night Stand

The One Night Stand

We were having a Monica "The First Night" song type of moment. Both of us sat on the sofa with space in between us. An episode of Chicago PD was on the television screen, but I wasn't paying attention to what was going on. My mind was on him, his good looks, his confidence, and his reasons for being here with me.

His name was Devonte and his confidence was my biggest problem. Earlier that night when he messaged me, it was like he wouldn't take no for an answer. Well, I couldn't say no to a man telling me to get dressed and hang with him. I thought about saying it several times. I thought about telling him never mind. He had just broken up with his ex-girlfriend and I didn't want to be a rebound. I also didn't want to fall into the trap of lust so soon after claiming I was abstaining from sex.

Then seeing him for the first time standing outside near his car waiting for me stirred something in my soul. I can't remember the last time I was able to hop in the passenger side of a man's car and have him take me wherever. I've always met up with men to stay in my comfort zone. I think I hugged him before getting in his car. I'm not sure. Nervousness had taken over my mind. Upon hopping in the car, I could smell the beer. Clearly I was dealing with a bad boy that wasn't afraid to drink and drive. He wasn't drunk or even tipsy though.

"Are you hungry?" Devonte asked.

Was I hungry? Before receiving his messages on Facebook that night, I was hungry. I was trying to choose between warming up leftovers in my fridge, sticking frozen foods into the oven, or cooking something on the stove. But then my hunger was replaced with curiosity.

"Nah," I said, "But I will be later."

We talked a little and sat in silence. I don't really know what kind of word flowed from my mouth.

"Are you thirsty?" he asked. I wasn't thirsty, but a drink could calm me down. He stopped at a gas station and we went in. I thought about grabbing cheap liquor, but instead went for a soda. After leaving the gas station, he drove little more. Then he mentioned getting a hotel room for the night.

"I'm thinking about getting a hotel room just to chill at for the night."

"Why?" I asked. "You have roommates?"

"Yeah, I live in a house with my father. I come and go as I please. If you wanted to go there, we can."

"Well, I live alone."

"In your apartment? No roommates? All by yourself?" He seemed surprised.

"Yeah." Devonte turned around and headed back to my place.

I couldn't believe I was inviting him in. Just a couple days ago I had told myself to take a break from men. My luck in the past few years had been men that only wanted casual sex, cheating men, long distance ones, and ones that were afraid to get from behind their computers and meet me in person. I knew I needed a break. I needed to breathe. I needed feminine energy around me, girl talks over drinks, laughing and sharing our joys and disappointments. The only women I could do that with were in other states and we were only communicating through the phone when our schedules happened to fall in sync. Instead of that desperately needed girl talk, I was putting myself in a position to have a new guy yearning for what was between my legs just so he could forget about me afterward.

Soon we were back at my place sitting on the sofa not paying attention to Chicago PD. Instead we were sitting in awkward silence, or asking questions just to have something to talk about, or even playing with our phones. I kept picking up my phone out of nervousness, but no one was texting me, or saying anything to me on social media.

"Come here." He pointed to his lap. It was then that I knew where we were heading.

"I'm interested in you," Devonte told me as he held me in his arms.

"I can tell."

"How?"

"This right here." Then we had our first kiss.

One minute we were in the living room and the next he had me on my bed. I have a habit of throwing jackets on it at the beginning of the day, so I pushed the jackets along with pillows onto the floor while he got undressed.

The sex started off new. I wasn't as relaxed as I should have been starting off and I didn't really know what to expect from him. But the more we got into it, the better it became. After the first round as we laid next to each other naked, catching our breaths, with only the light of the television highlighting our brown skinned bodies, I realized I didn't know the man laying next to me.

It was like Tamia's song, "There's a Stranger In My House," except he was adoring me. He was lusting after me and I was returning the lust, but at the same time still trying to figure out why I was chosen. Plus he really was a stranger.

Well before that night we had chatted through the Facebook messenger a few times. I had looked through his pictures and read some of his status updates. I did know a little about him.

Wait, this guy wasn't just a random Facebook friend that turned into a random hookup. I ended up requesting him, because his crazy girlfriend didn't understand that you don't ask new women to appear in your cheating man's eyesight. Or maybe I should have just stuck with my original intentions of speaking with her and never connected with her cheating man on social media.

The Beginning

"Hey, since we're in the same city, we should get together sometimes for drinks and discuss business plans." I meant what I was saying, but I wasn't sure Avery was for real about discussing anything dealing with business.

"Okay, sure. Are you busy Saturday?" Avery asked.

"Saturday is perfect. Just let me know what time."

It was supposed to be friendly conversation in the Facebook messenger that would somehow lead to business talk between women. However, that Saturday meeting would never happen. Avery wasn't as serious about furthering her career as me. She was too busy focusing on men, or one man to be exact. We had spent our conversations discussing the headaches we had gotten while attempting to make potentially great men our on. I was okay with that route of conversation, because I had already put everything I told her about in a book. But I wanted to talk about more than men.

I had done it plenty of times before using Facebook messenger, the Instagram DM, and even the Twitter DM. Many women that I had never been face to face with had exchanged messages with me discussing our dreams of making money off of our passions. Sometimes they were conversations with men, because men have dreams too. This always started with personal information about ourselves being exchanged, because creative entrepreneurs usually use their personal lives to help enhance their story telling. Maybe in this situation we went a little too personal and that was why it was hard to get to the professional part.

Earlier in the conversation we were discussing her issues with her man. His name was Devonte.

"Girl, he's perfect for me. Even though I already have kids, I've already told him how many more I want."

"Really?" I said. "How long have you two been dating?"

"About two months, but there are some issues with him."

"Like what?"

"He keeps talking to all these women. I've taken his phone and deleted numbers out of it. I've also gone through his social media and blocked women that were messaging him."

"WOW!" I responded, but I was really thinking that's a lot of work to do for a man you've only been with a short period of time.

"Listen, he's currently blocked me on Facebook because I blocked all those women. Will you do me a favor and request him? I need someone to let me know what he's posting."

I shouldn't have done it. I was still in a very vulnerable place emotionally from the last man I had dealt with. He wasn't my man, but he was a single man that couldn't make up his mind whether he wanted to be in a loving relationship or just occasionally getting great sex. So I settled for great sex until I was tired of him.

I sent the friend request like Avery asked, glanced at his profile, and sent a screenshot of his latest Facebook status to her. That status was all about her and what she had done. She wrote an "lol" and was satisfied.

Were they really in a relationship? It was hard to tell because these two were so dysfunctional. I didn't need to know much about them. Avery had already said she was going through his phone and social media messages. Even though he was cheating on her, she was determined to hold onto him. However, he didn't seem like he was having the same emotions for her. Soon after sending that friend request, he sent me a message.

"Hey, so what made you request me?"

"Avery was talking about you, so I decided to send a request. What's up with you and her anyway?"

"We've tried being together, but she's too much drama for me. She just does a lot that I can't handle."

"Oh, I understand." Then I went on to tell Devante the same story about the previous man that I had told Avery and many others. I should have reported the conversation to Avery since I was supposed to be a spy for her, but I never did. I just thought of it as a quick conversation.

We never talked again until that very random night that he messaged me on Facebook about hanging out. It was a Thursday, cold outside, and my mind was in a world of it's own.

It Went Too Far

After that night, Devante became just another nigga on my hit list. However, it took him some time to realize that. For several days after that he asked when we would hook up again. I wasn't in a rush to see him, so I wasn't giving him an answer.

At the same time Avery started acting like a regular single woman again. She would update statuses directed at men not acting right, jump in groups to flirt in the comments section, and post pictures trying to get attention from anyone. I was no longer talking to her. I had no intention of telling her about that night with her man and we had nothing to discuss since she had clearly forgotten about the business meeting. However, she did eventually find out that I spoke with him.

My number was saved in Devante's phone. On one random Saturday a little over a week later I decided to call him. My call went unanswered. A few days after that they were back together and she decided to make a very public Facebook status about seeing someone on her friends list saved in her man's phone. Well, she called her ex-man in the status.

"I was going through my ex-man phone

and saw a missed phone call from someone on my friend list on it.

You just can't trust people smh."

I kept quiet and read the comments. Avery was really embarrassing herself by admitting she was still spending time with a man that couldn't be trusted. I knew it wasn't over though. Eventually we would have to disconnect from each other on all social media platforms. It would be better for both of us. I was also done with Devante.

Another week went by. Neither of them were on my mind. I had checked a day before to remove Avery from my friends list, but her profile was nowhere to be found. It was a Tuesday night and I was getting ready for bed when my phone rang.

I didn't recognize the number. I should have ignored it, but instead I answered.

"Hello?"

"Hey." I heard a man's voice.

"Hi, who is this?"

"Devante," he said.

"Oh," I said shocked. I had planned on never seeing or speaking to him again. But I also wasn't ready to talk to him at that moment. I made up an excuse about getting ready for bed. He said okay and we decided we would speak again at a better time. No time would be better though.

What I did do to officially close out that chapter of my life with those two was send him the story I had written about that night with him. After he read it I explained I was working on a book and his story would be featured in it. He was cool with it.

But it still wasn't over yet. A day later I received one more message from Devante's Facebook page. He didn't write it though. It was Avery. The messaged said:

"Bitch Leave My Man Alone You Dirty Hoe."

The following is the poem I wrote after everything happened. I stopped communicating with both. Even thought we were no longer in communication, she had informed a lot of people that I had slept with her ex. It was Women's History Month. While women were being celebrated, the message saying, "Bitch leave my man alone you dirty hoe," was still floating through my mind. Her friends laughing and calling me names all because she wanted the world to know that I slept with her ex disturbed my spirit. I wasn't feeling like a good friend when writing the following. I wasn't even feeling like a woman that a man would really be interested in. However, this moment had become a part of my life and I was trying to figure out a way to accept it.

Dirty Feminism

It wasn't love. Just one night I found myself alone with this sexy man. One thing led to another and we moved too fast.

But we weren't even a perfect match!

Clouded by lust, still high off the sex, I forgot to let him know to keep it on the down low. Nobody was supposed to know about how I acted like a hoe. How while having the same exact desire as him, I gave him what he wanted.

While barely knowing anything about him, I quickly took off my clothes. Clearly he was a fuck boy, only in my home in hopes of getting sex, but yet I willingly gave a little bit of myself.

Other men were given chances with me and I was hoping maybe he would be different. He would consider my feelings and not be another trail of hurt. He wasn't the one though. In return I got a moment of pleasure and a stain on my reputation.

Was he single? Was he still in a relationship? I believed what he said.

Was I in the wrong for saying yes? I was usually a no girl. No I don't want to go on that date. Nah, you can't come to my house. Umm, sorry I'm busy on all of those days.

But for some reason I said okay. Now they know about Lashuntrice. They know I like the sex, and sometimes I move too fast, and I'm still choosing the wrong men. They know that if I'm not publicly claiming a man, then I must be someone's secret lover. Good enough for him to fuck, but not good enough to be seen out in public with.

But even worse, they know I'll screw over any woman for a chance with a man, even if that woman is a friend. Who cares if they just broke up five seconds ago or five years ago? This could be my chance.

And they've decided I have broken pussy.

Pussy that gets played with a few times and tossed to the side of the road for the next man to stumble upon.

Damn, am I really not good enough?

There have been times I hesitantly gave my body to a man, wasn't really sure I could trust him, couldn't even remember if we held hands…but I listened to his words, believed him when he said the sex would be good.

And there have been moments I didn't think twice about the man I was allowing in my bed. All I knew was that I wanted his kisses to be soft, and his touch to be gentle, and if he ever got a little rough with me, left me physically sore, he'd care enough to want to ease my pain.

But I've also had moments where I didn't tell friends about my sexual experiences. Whether good or bad, I wanted to live in the moment, no questions of who the man was; no judgment of whether I was right or wrong. I just wanted to be confident in the womanly decision had I made.

Well I've made my decision and now I have a new label.

At one point I was just a girl, nothing more. Then I was friend, someone's friend. Several people's friend until one day someone saw me as a nerd. I was book smart, so I was labeled an outcast until I became a woman. My body changed, someone thought I had a nice shape. Is attractive a label? Well men started to take interest in me. Men noticed me, and it felt good. Then someone noticed me enough to give me the title of I of girlfriend. After girlfriend every woman wants to move up to the title of wife, but instead I've been labeled a hoe.

 Because I reckless with my femininity, attracting the attention of a man another woman desperately wanted, hurting her feelings in the process I have to claim this new title.

 Girl! Friend! Nerd! Woman! Attractive! Girlfriend! Hoe! Not yet a Wife! Those are the titles that define me.

Death Of Me

People are gonna be the death of me

Everyone and their different personalities will one day drive

me crazy

The happy

Sad

Mad

The talkative

Know-It-Alls

Stubborn

Quiet

Emotionless

The crybabies

And all other kinds are gonna work my nerves until they

explode and send me into a pit of rage unlike no other

And it will happen so suddenly I won't be able to explain my

actions

Maybe its because I've because I'm too nice

Always agreeing with everyone else

I haven't spoken up for myself enough

I keep too many things bottled in

Or maybe it'll be a totally different reason

But it will be such a scene doctors and nurses will be called in

to strap me down and drug me up and put me in a deep slumber

so when I wake up four walls is all I will see

And then the rest of my days I'll find myself alone

But the personalities of all these damn people for all These

damn years will be stuck in my head and have me so far gone

that people….

I can still remember back in high school when this guy decided

to call me ugly and continually tease me

I don't know why

I was always minding my own business

And everyone usually left me alone

But he insisted on bothering me

And no one stood up for me until one day I started to cry

I think his name was Thomas

And I've met a million men like him since then

And I can still remember my first best friend

She also became my first enemy

She flirted with a boy she knew I had a crush on

And she did it because she knew I was too shy to speak up

Later on she would threaten to kill me

And then cut herself when I no longer wanted to be her friend

And it happened in a classroom full of people

Clearly she was crazy

But her crazy must have been contagious

Because I can still remember

And the memories will manage to be the death of me

Joan Clayton

I wanna be like Joan when I grow up

I'm already in my 30's

She was in her 30's the first time I started paying attention to
her

She'd already climbed the ladder of success

As I see a lack of funds in my bank account I think about her

I believe she was a lawyer trying to become a partner at the law
firm

And she had her own home

A home she opened up to her friends

And she could easily get a man

So she was never alone

And she showed a black girl like me that you can always quit
working for a boss

And still successfully survive

Of course that is if your friends have your back

She taught me that friendship is a bond worth having

From the beginning she introduced me to a group of friends I

wished I had

And now I can follow her lead

Become successful

And build unbreakable bonds

Claire and Raven Too

I always wanted to be like Claire

She was stylish

Her clothes and hair were always on point

She was pretty

Makeup always done just right

From head to toe she knew how to shine

And who better to imitate from my days of growing up

Well I always wanted to be like Raven too

She had her own style

And she was clearly mature for her age

I felt mature for my age

We were only a year apart

But my parents said I couldn't be like her

I had to stay in a child's place

So now I'm trying to play catch-up

Be more like them during a time where ordinary girls like me

can finally be something special

I'm not a television star though

So I use social media to spread my message

Posting the same pictures and texts on

Facebook, Instagram and Twitter

I hope someone's noticing

I need comments

I need likes

Because I'm trying to be a star

Trying to sell a product

A product that just happens to be myself

SENDING MY SIMILARITIES

If I could mail my thoughts right to you, I would

I'd place them in a cute little package

And make sure your name is highlighted

You won't initially know it's from me

But when you finally open it

I hope you'll open it

You'll discover that we are not that much different

See I've been trying to talk to you

I can tell you're a cool person

Fun to hang with

But still motivational at the right times

And you'd fit well into my inner circle

But the shy girl in me keeps quiet

I don't know how I'll ever make new friends

Every time I come close to it, shit happens

Someone finds something wrong with me

And I can tell you're also looking for that imperfection

Can you trust me? I'm too quiet for you to trust

I can't dance

You think it's funny and brush me off

Someone hates me because I have something they want

You take their side and eventually forget I exist

Yet I still try to get your attention

What's wrong with me?

I recognize we are different people

We have different mindsets

Mines involves seeing people as real in the beginning

Yet we have similar needs

We need to be trusted

We need to be cared about

And we have similar experiences that have broken

us

I want you to see that I am trustworthy

I want you to see that I have been broken

So I put it in package to mail off to you

Hopefully you open it

And find out that we are more alike than your initial thoughts

BREAK ME DOWN

I wish you could understand

How much you break me down

I keep telling you what I've accomplished

A college degree

Self published author

The ability to live paycheck to paycheck

And enough bravery to be able to travel alone

I keep telling you what I'm going to do

One day I'll be someone's boss

And one day I'll have a family of my own

Not once have I asked for your help

Just a little support

But instead you have a lot of advice

I hear your criticism

You don't like my work

You say it's too personal

And personal is just not your style

And your attack my looks

I just don't look good enough for you

I'm too skinny

And my clothes are too revealing

If I give you the opportunity

You'll turn me into a brand new woman

But since I'm not doing that you'd rather leave me alone

I wait for your positive views

Can you find anything nice to say?

I pretend like you don't faze me

But deep down inside I'm hurting

You're so lost in yourself

You probably never realized I cry

But the tears I've become good at hiding

Throwing Shade

Sorry I'm not like you

I'm trying to better myself

Chasing my dreams

I dream of being someone people can admire

Sorry I'm not like you

I'm chasing after the better man

Not settling for sharing

Not settling for sneaking through phones

Or checking social media for messages to other women

I'm selfish

But I'm not trying to change him

I only want a man with the same mentality

Sorry I'm not like you

I'm trying to live my best life

Explore my city and beyond

Creating memories others could never imagine

Allowing myself to dream

Not getting stuck in my current situation

Sorry I'm not like you

I want to see others happy

Hear about their great achievements

Find out what's next in life

Not discourage them because I'm unhappy

Not silence them because their good vibes makes me feel
insecure

Sorry I'm not like you

And I'm not gonna call you out

I'm not trying to be you

Just gonna brush your negativity off

And continue to make plans for my life

Girl ain't nobody hating on you

I want to see the same thing in you that I'm looking for in
myself

So chill with talking about me behind my back

No one believes you anyway

And chill with trying to start one-sided beefs

Because I'm not about to argue with you

But if you want some help getting your self esteem

You know where to find me

ARROGANT

I try to blend in

Interact in the online groups you add me to

Be involved in the messy group chats you create

Put laughing emojis on the memes you find so funny

I try to be your friend

Show up to the parties you claim are lit

Be your designated driver so you don't hold back on the liquor

Extend invitations even when I just want to be Alone

Be there for you even when you're obsessed

With cutting everyone off

But the truth is the groups are stupid

The people are messy

You are messy

And the messiness is draining

And the memes have never been funny

I'm trying to be cool with you

See I'm not a mean person

But hanging with you is tiring

You're never even there for me

But you get mad when I can't be there for you

Seriously I'm better than that

And I'm better than you

GOT MY OWN

I'm out of your league,

I got my own.

Rent, car, electronics, water,

Everything's in my name

Even the bed I sleep on, I own.

Been a good girl all my life.

Worked hard for this damn degree.

Made sure to stay out of trouble.

My records are clean.

Corporate America keeps me stressed.

But continually striving for growth keeps me blessed

I'm a nice person

But I'm not the friend you can verbally abuse

I'm not the one you can take advantage of

I'm not the side chick or the main chick

I'm not your little freak

I'm not out here to please you

I'm here to take care of me

So respect me as I am

Or you make room for people who will

I'm not the one you should be making your enemy

Part 2

LIKE MAYA ANGELOU AND MAYA WILKES

Dress falling off my shoulders

Barely sober

How did I get here with you

I don't know

But tonight is the night

I'm gonna tell you all about my dreams

One day I'll be famous

Cameras flashing all around me

Like Maya Angelou

Little children and grown adults will repeat my words

Like Maya Wilkes

One day I'll be selling books on a street corner in Hollywood

No label

No agent

Right now you're my only fan

So I'm showing you my talent

Can I sing for you?

Excuse me if I don't sound good

Can I dance for you?

The tequila got me a little clumsy

Catch me if I fall

And whatever happens next

That can be my next poem

BELONGING TO THE WORLD

I knew you'd fucked up other girls

Broken a few hearts

Didn't even feel sorry when the tears fell

Tears are just an effect of the game you play

But that didn't stop me from getting you too

Believing I could be different to you

I fell victim to your aggression

Getting lost in your words of seduction

Remember that time you said you wanted to fuck me insane?

And in that area I had no complaints

But I also liked that you talked grown man shit

You were working on getting your savings up

Always thinking about making better money

You talked about continuously filling out job applications

I admired you for your persistence to grow

But what I didn't realize is I didn't fit into your equation

I daydreamed of us one day having grown together

The money was right

Kids were in the picture

We had created our own family traditions

Instead of my vision, I found I was just a momentary freaky

obsession

"We're just having fun," you said

And before I could process you were already moving on

But what the next woman hadn't realized yet is

You're not hers either

DANGEROUS WOMAN

What do you want?

What are you here for?

Is it love?

Is it lust?

Because I can be the woman of your dreams

I'd do everything you ask for

Whether it's be a traditional wife

What do you want for dinner tonight?

Or you wanna go half on all the bills

But sometimes I'll be too tired for sex

Or we could be friends with benefits

But our unemotional sex can only go on for so long

Or we could make a good one night stand

Two strangers meeting in the night

And years later when you think of me it'll feel like a dream

But you have to choose an option
Because I'm only giving you what you ask for

I can be warm and loving if that's what you want
Romantic dates is part of my goal
We'll cuddle when it's just the two of us
And sometimes cuddle when others are around

I can be clingy if you're looking for the stalker type
I'll be up under you all day and night
I'll even search your phone and social media
Make sure you're not talking to any other women
I'm not the trusting type

Or I can be wintertime cold
You wanted the sex and got it
Why are you speaking to me again?

CUM FOR ME

How do I make you cum for me?

I know I'm one of several women you've been With

I can feel your experience when we're doing it

I know I'm not the best you've had

One of those women gave you better head

And another got on top and made you cum real

Quick

And let's not forget the women in porn that turn You on

But I'm also not trying to compete

My goal isn't the best sex

It's that you feel me

You get lost in me

You find yourself within me

You like what you see

You like how I feel

And it makes you feel good

Can you see us together for a while?

I'm not gonna say forever

I understand for you that's too much pressure

So let's do this in baby steps

I'll let you decide when to make us official

It could be a month from now

Or we could take two years to see how we feel Together

And I'll definitely skip over the topic of

Marriage

If it means having you around,

We can be like Oprah and Stedman

Just with a little less money

So how do I make you stay with me?

Because I'm not about to settle for polygamy or Cheating

And if there's another woman fighting for you,

And it's a hard decision

You have to choose

You better choose me

LOCATION

Hey Baby… what's your name?

I wanna know your location

I'm a little shy so… excuse me if I move too fast

I'm trying to ride your vibrations

Cause you're 6'5

Brown eyes

As fine as it gets

And I'm not waiting for the next woman to get your attention

Want you all to myself

So let's ensure that we get to know each other well

We can have… long phone conversations

Or just listen to each other breathe

We can Netflix and chill

I think you're the one

I'll give all my femininity to you

GROWN

(Shout out to the Facebook friend that inspired my anniversary of the third date line.)

I'm trying to grow up

I'm trying to fall in love

I've been stuck in a childhood routine for so long

From classes everyone said I needed to take

To a work schedule I must always obey

I switched from being dependent

To paying bills on my own

But it's only because I was doing what I was Told

But what about Love?

That's reserved for someone that's grown

Sweet prince of the ghetto

Will you help me feel more like a woman?

Because last night I had a dream about you

In the dream you were making love to me

And you kept telling me how much you missed me

And even though we had taken those vows that we would be together

During any moment we were spending apart I was missing you too

It came after we had a romantic outing together

We were celebrating the anniversary of our 3rd date Together

You wanted to make the night special

So you showed up with flowers and candy

And then we enjoyed a nice picnic in the park

And the stars even came out and shined bright

But now that I'm awake I can tell

Like a kid with ADHD

 I only have half your attention

Do you think one day you can love me?

Because I'm working on growing up

They say getting my period is when I transition From a little girl to a woman

They say losing my virginity puts me one step Closer to womanhood

They say womanhood has been achieved once I'm in the world

of student loans and paychecks That are never enough

But even when I have all that experience behind me

I still look for my womanhood within your eyes

Can you see my maturity?

HEARTBEAT

We finish having passionate sex

The temperature in the room goes up

But that's not enough to separate us

As we lay on the bed we cuddle up

Your right arm is wrapped around me

I lay my head on your chest
I can hear your heartbeat

I can feel the way you're breathing

You're comfortable

I know it's because of me

OVERSTIMULATED

Darkness outside

A random movie on the television screen

The smell of smoke fills the air

A black and mild is in your hand

Light from the nearby lamp illuminates your Body as you lean

back in the chair

No clothes on

Your brown skin is waiting for my touch

It's time for me to please you

I'm on my knees

Looking into your eyes

As you look into mine

With my mouth I do my best

I have to turn you on

I'm wet

It's time to combine our bodies in the most intimate way

We start on the couch

And move to the bed

I'll never forget the feeling of you carrying me while

you're still inside of me

Our bodies are in synch

We develop a rhythm

Sounds come out of our mouths

Then we explode with pleasure at the same time

Is it hot in here or is it just me?

SEXUALITY & VULNERABILITY

I allow you into my life

I convince myself that I need you

It's the best way to make myself learn you

Then I run to someone else for a listening ear

I need to release the feelings

I need to let someone

Anyone

Know about the issues

Know about the feelings of doubts

And the feelings of curiosity

That you're creating inside of me

I allow you to hold me

Even if only for a moment in time

Please don't rush it

I'm assuming that sex is what's really on your Mind

But lets stay in this position for a minute more

Your arms around me

Wherever our bodies meet

Cuddled on the couch

Or in the bed

Or even right before you leave

So later on I can tell my friends how warm you Made me feel

I dress up for you

Even if the destination is to nowhere

You've told me which dress is your favorite

You've helped me pick lingerie you'd love to see me In

Do you see me trying to look good for you?

I strip for you

The clothes are on the floor

The pillows are pushed off the bed

There's R&B music playing

Isley Brothers Between The Sheets sets the mood

I create intimacy with you

It's not just about us getting naked

Or how many different sex positions we can do

It's about how we make each other feel when We're together

It's about how we are still feeling when we're Apart

I feel sexy when it comes to you

You've made it clear that you love my body

But I'm also scared

Is this love real?

Or will you be the next man to hurt me?

The next man to run off with parts of me?

Those emotions are what make me feminine

What makes me beautiful

I'm vulnerable

And I want to hide it until we get this connection just Right

But instead I talk about our memories

I reveal special moments to friends

And talk about my feelings to strangers

And I use you to still feel love even if it isn't real love

48 HOURS

It's been 4 hours since you've left
I should be asleep but I can't stop thinking about you
There's something you don't know
Something I should have told you before that first kiss
For about 24 to 48 hours after we do this you're my man
I expect to see that look in your eyes that says even though you
don't wanna leave, you have to

It's been 14 hours and I haven't heard a word from you
You took too long to say something so I sent a text instead
We shouldn't be making this awkward
I'm not a prostitute
Remember how I told you to study every inch of my body
while it was in front of you
The way my breasts perked up as you sucked on them
We came together for pleasure, not money

24 hours have passed
Have you forgotten about me already?

I'm trying to focus on something else

But I can still feel your hands gripping my hips as you hit it

from the back

Please don't disappear

Don't be the typical fuck boy

Waiting a week or two

Then calling again for more

48 hours something tells me we ain't gonna last

I've gotten my gangsta back

And now I remember you just wanted to be another nigga on

my hit list

You didn't have to say it

But it's showing in your lack of actions

72 hours you're horny and ready to repeat this cycle of emotions

all over again

COME THROUGH AND CHILL

Just say you will come through and chill

And tonight we won't be just friends

Only a little awkward conversation

Hey, how have you been?

I'm fine and you?

As I start to strip

The sight of your sexiness has it hot in here

Do you feel that?

It's my body ready for yours

Are you ready for me?

If we do this, it'll be a new beginning

Because my goal is to make you cum

And then keep coming back again

So how do we start off?

Nice and slow

I'm ready to take my time

Putting my hands in places of yours that I've never seen

Or do you wanna be rough right away

Slap it in my face and shove it down my throat

Either way I'll never see you the same

So pick up the phone

Show me that it's real

I know that you've been watching me

In my mind I can tell you've been talking about me

So let's do it

Fuck all night

And afterwards we'll make our new situation official

THE DAY YOU MARRY ME

Can you picture it?

Me in a beautiful white dress

You standing at the alter waiting for me to come down the aisle

We've made it this far in our relationship

At first I thought you were a mistake

There was no courting

I gave myself to you to easily

Then I pretended you might just be a friend

Even if you were coming back for only a few benefits

But we've been doing this for a minute

And I don't want to let you go

My feelings for you run too deep

So can you imagine yourself reciting vows to me?

For better or worse

You better not cheat on me

In sickness and in health

I'll be your nurse when you need me

And I'll play nurse just for fun

And of course you have to do the same for me

This is not a game

Can you imagine yourself putting me first?

Treating me like the amazing woman I am

Especially if you want me to have your kid

And even if you never want children

You still have to cater to my heart's desires

Currently all I need from you is love

Lusting

Lusting after you like Nicole and Boris on Soulfood

Trying to get to know you like a best friend

Trying to set appointments with you like a job interview

Trying to get close to you like the covers on my bed

Trying to catch feelings for you like Drake has for Keke

I know we just saw each other earlier, but baby are you missing me yet?

Fantasizing about wearing your clothes so when you're not around I can still feel your presence

Thinking about ways to be spontaneous so our chemistry will stay fresh

Planning to grow with you like Denzel and Pauletta

Reminiscing about the times we've already had

ABOUT THE AUTHOR

Lashuntrice Bradley was born in Plant City, Florida and raised in Houston, Texas. She fell in love with books at a young age, but she was able to explore her passion for writing upon becoming a student at Florida A&M University in 2005. After graduating with a journalism degree and no journalism job in place, she started blogging to continue working on her passion for writing. Her goal is to open her heart, entertain you, and share incredibly relate-able stories.

For more information visit her website www.searchinformystar.com.

www.ingramcontent.com/pod-product-compliance
Lightning Source LLC
Chambersburg PA
CBHW032212040426
42449CB00005B/562